Venice

Domenico Crivellari

Venice

Electa

Translation
Huw Evans

Filmsetting of the text
and reproduction of the illustrations
by Bassoli Olivieri Prestampa,
Milan

Printed in Italy
© 1993 by **Electa**, Milan
Elemond Editori Associati

Contents

The origins

The long road that would lead Venice to the heights of political and economic power commenced in the 5th and 6th centuries A.D. and was the summation, as in all human affairs, both individual and collective, of favourable opportunities, the capacity to adapt to a geographical environment that presented unusual advantages but considerable drawbacks too, and of lucky coincidences.

In the 5th century the lagoon was very different from the one we know today: what see now is the result of the unceasing activity of man and nature.

No urban form, just a few scattered islands: along the islands still existing and inhabited today (Murano, Burano, Mazzorbo) were others that have now disappeared (Ammiana, Costanziaca), engulfed by the lagoon, and others, like Torcello, harshly treated by nature, that have gone into decline after a long period of splendour.

Here, on this margin of the land, lived a sparse population whose activities centred around the salt-pans, fishing, patches of cultivation and trade. They used boats with flat keels and of low tonnage that were built specially for navigation on the channels of the lagoon and which were dragged over the most difficult stretches with ropes. This embryo of the future fleet that was to plough all the known seas already permitted the maintenance of precarious links with the coast of Istria on the other side of the Adriatic, and was able to move up the courses of the rivers.

Accounts of Venetian history written after the year 1000, such as the chronicles of Martino da Canal and the doge Andrea Dandolo, embroidered this period with fantastic

*Drawings of early
14th-century Venetian ships.
From "Zibaldone Da Canal".
New Haven, Yale University
Library.*

episodes of mythical date, like that of the 25th March 421, the day of the city's foundation, and with glorious military victories in battles that were never fought; legends that ennobled the origins of a by now famous Venice, in the manner typical of every parvenu.

Hence there were two supporting pillars of the incipient economic growth: transport by sea and river, which presupposed a plentiful supply of timber and a high degree of technical skill and led to the development of a large fleet already capable of covering remarkable distances; and salt, which required equipment for its extraction and means of transport.

The salt, much in demand and a cash-commodity par excellence in the early Middle Ages, could be bartered by the Venetians for the foodstuffs that could not be grown on the islands. The date emblematic of the start of economic and social development in the future Venice should however be set around 568-569, when the Longobard invasions, even more bloody and resolute than earlier ones, finally drove the coastal populations to take refuge in greater numbers in the lagoon.

From 570 until the end of the 7th century however, the Venetians, both native and immigrant, enjoyed a period of relative calm, allowing them to make peaceful progress with their characteristic activities.

Each island had come to adopt its own social organization, which doubtless must have reproduced the pattern of the coastal town from which its population had originated. In periods of peace contacts were resumed with these towns, property was reclaimed and rights re-established on the lands so precipitously abandoned.

Among the islands stood out Cittanova, founded by refugees from Oderzo and which became the political capital in the course of the 7th century, and Torcello, the economic capital and seat of a "magnum emporium" whose fame spread beyond the bounds of the lagoon. The see of Altino was transferred here in 635 and in 639 work was begun on the construction of the cathedral church, which has survived to this day despite radical alterations.

The fundamental cause behind a centuries-long period little troubled by war lay in the fact that the archipelago had become a frontierpost between the two superpowers of the day, the Longobards and the Byzantines. While the latter strived to maintain the status quo, preoccupied as they were by Arab pressure to the east, the former were slowly assimilating local habits and customs, eventually converting to Catholicism. Out of this was born a tacit pact of nonbelligerence which permitted both adversaries to establish greater political control over their own realms. So it was that towards the end of the 7th century Byzantium had to pay greater attention to the military and bureaucratic organization of the islands, according to the pattern followed in all parts of the empire, i.e. by entrusting civil powers as well to the local militias.

In accordance with this directive, the magister militium,

Paulicius, was installed in 697 in the "capital" Cittanova, establishing a decentralized tribunate, but one that was dependent on Ravenna.

According to later accounts and by long custom Paulicius has been looked on as the first doge. This tradition aimed, not at historical accuracy, but to stress the sovereignty of the people of the islands, and their autonomy, which it tried to date further back in time. The advent of Leo III Isauricus to the throne of Byzantium in 717 unleashed on the empire a crusade against the use of a classic Christian devotion: that of images. This provoked a violent quarrel between the Papacy and the Empire, the breaking of one alliance and the formation of a new one between the Papacy and a new actor that strode domineeringly onto the Italian stage: the dynasty of the Carolingians. It was fairly easy to predict that the anti-Byzantine factions present on the islands would seize the opportunity to proclaim the independence of the "province": the killing of Paulicius, an obligatory step in the assertion of the new course, brought to the fore Orso, the leader of the rebels, who was proclaimed "dux". Orso, by full right of history, was the first elected doge. The year – 727 – may be considered the second emblematic moment in the history of nascent Venice. The birth of the dogal magistracy, which was to survive for 1,070 years under Orso's 117 successors, found its legitimacy in the assumption of autonomous political power, even though its prerogatives and functions would undergo

Procurator of Saint Mark, from the "Codex Grevembroch". Museo Correr.

Doges' Palace, Porta della Carta, detail.

Lazzaro Bastiani, Portrait of Doge Francesco Foscari. Museo Correr.

Translation of the Body of Saint Mark, detail. Saint Mark's Basilica, portal of Sant'Alipio.

profound transformations before settling into the definitive order of the state organization. But this would not occur until the end of the 13th century. Orso's achievement, however, was not definitive; nor was the separation of the Venetians from Byzantium. Violent agitations succeeded one another over the brief span of the following decades. The date 811 marks a third important step in the birth of Venice, chronologically the third such date, after 568-569, the years of the migratory explosion with its social transformations, and 727 which marked the accession of the doge Orso and the beginning of effective political autonomy. On Rialto, as if to mark the irreversibility of the choice made, work was immediately begun on the construction of the Palace that was to be the seat of the doge, though with many alterations and enlargements, for almost a millenium. Another event a few years later was to give definitive sanction to this choice: the finding of the body of St. Mark and its enshrinement in the chapel adjoining the Palace. The cult of St. Mark was very soon to supplant that of Theodore and become a potent vehicle of patriotism. For centuries Venetian soldiers would cry "Mark, Mark" before battle in foreign lands and on remote seas, as if to invoke their far-off homeland. The winged lion, symbol of the saint, was to make its appearance in every part of the world, as a symbol of Venice itself, and for five centuries Venetian gold ducats would bear the effigy of St. Mark in the act of handing the standard to the doge.

In 829 construction of the chapel adjoining the palace was begun. Here the relics were enshrined, placed significantly under the protection of the doge to strengthen further

the position of the still narrow space between the small square and the lagoon as the centre of the dogate. The island of Rialto asserted greater and greater authority as the centre of the whole insular settlement, continuing a process of urbanization that became more marked at the beginning of the 10th century.

A social stratification was established with the *maiores* at the top, rich proprietors of lands and salt-pans who also practised mercantile activities, and beneath them the *mediocres*, i.e. the salt workers, fishermen, boat builders, sailors and artisans – among whom glass-workers were already to be found –, a population dedicated to part-time activity, whose fundamental objective was that of procuring their daily means of subsistence. At the bottom came the *minores*, who in part carried out with less success and in a more marginal manner the activities of the *mediocres* and in part depended more directly on the *maiores*. As is obvious and happens in every place and every time, the will of the latter was soon decisive in political matters as well.

Turkish Ambassador. From the "Codex Grevembroch". Museo Correr.

As the myth of social equality claimed by later historical accounts is no longer credible today, it is very difficult to lend credence to the literature on the rôle of the *concio* – the assembly of the entire population – that was supposed to have played an active and decision-making part in the election of the doges and in the most important choices in the life of those days. There is a hagiographic tendency always to see more democracy in the past than in the present and above all more democracy than was in fact exercised, as if the most evolved forms of civilized life might be found by looking backwards in history.

Once the seat of government had been shifted to Rialto and the *concio* was held in the small square facing the Palace and the chapel of San Marco, which had by this time become the "seat of power", the lowest-class inhabitants of the islands scattered throughout the lagoon soon ceased to participate, leaving the field free to the *maiores* and the people of Rialto. The assembly was thus transformed into a *placito*: no longer a meeting of all the free men of the dogate – who rarely assembled and then only to ratify decisions already taken – but of their representatives, selected by the administration through a procedure that must be considered rather suspect. This process would lead, on the threshold of the 14th century, to this class, through the "locking of the Great Council", becoming a closed caste, the exclusive proprietor of the Venetian state. Until then, however, the social system retained a certain elasticity as well as an upward mobility for all those who made consistent profits from trade. The *maiores* were not yet a closed group but were open to the *nouveaux riches*. Among the latter, the Ziani and Mastropietro families would be able to raise one of their sons to the dogate in the second half of the 12th century. So the key to social success was wealth, but not so much the secure wealth of real estate as the more profitable and dynamic one that derived from trade and from transport by river and by sea.

The period of greatest development

The period that stretches from 1200 to 1500 is considered the one in which the trade, international influence and form of internal government of Venice all reached the height of their development.

After 1000 the whole of Italy experienced, at least until 1348 – the year in which the Black Death spread through all the countries of Europe leaving a third of the population dead in its wake – a period of rapid renewal. The small manufacturing industries were supported by an expanding commercial organization that went from strength to strength, monetary exchange returned to replace barter and there was rapid growth in agriculture thanks to the introduction of technical improvements and the triennial rotation of crops.

At once cause and effect of the improvements in all sectors of economic life was the demographic growth; according to reliable estimates the population of Italy, which was around 5 million in the year 1000, had grown to 11 million by about 1300 and similar increases were recorded among other major European populations. The cities began to bloom and fill with people once more and their demographic growth is still visible today in the successive enlargements of city walls. "The commercial revolution", as the rapid growth of Italian commerce has been called, found an important vehicle in the Crusades, which after 1100 drove the Christian world to the conquest of the Holy Land. The major Italian naval powers – Genoa, Pisa and Venice in chronological order – supplied ships, arms and provisions to the crusaders and permitted them to set up true territorial dominions in the coastal cities of Syria and Palestine.

In exchange for their collaboration the maritime cities were conceded quarters warehouses and markets in all the principal ports and the cities of the hinterland.

These territories enjoyed the full rights of political and commercial extra-territoriality with privileges far superior to those that the various decrees of the Byzantine emperor had already guaranteed the Venetians and to a lesser extent the Genoese. So deep a penetration into the countries of the Levant also opened up new possibilities for access to trade with the distant lands of Asia and of the Indies. For Venice all this meant the growth and expansion of her own potential to reach the whole eastern part of the Mediterranean basin. She found herself in a privileged and favoured position, having established the pre-conditions for this accelerated and impetuous growth over the preceding centuries. But the definitive turning-point came with the 4th Crusade, instigated by Venice herself in 1202, in which the doge Enrico Dandolo took part. The doge was eighty years old and blind but he had a past record as a valiant military leader.

The conquest of Constantinople put the formal seal on the end of Venice's subordination to the Eastern Empire, a vassalage that had in fact ceased the century before with the establishment of Venice's naval and military power and had been transformed, as we have seen, into a rela-

Side page
Gentile Bellini, Saint Mark preaching in Alexandria, detail. Milan, Pinacoteca di Brera.

*Jean Leclerc, Doge Enrico
Dandolo swearing the Pacts
in Saint Mark's, detail.
Doges' Palace, sala
del Maggior Consiglio.*

*Lazzaro Bastiani, Doges
Antonio Venier and Michele
Steno. Museo Correr.*

tionship of alliance. The conquests of territory were oriented towards trade and a true empire of naval bases was established. At the same time, either through commercial agreements or through free-trade zones in the areas controlled by the crusaders, other bases were set up in the Mediterranean at Tunis, Alexandria in Egypt, Jaffa, Acre, Antioch in Syria and Tana, situated on the Sea of Azov, a strategic point of primary importance for the overland route to China. The European occupation of Constantinople lasted about fifty years. In the July of 1261 Michael Palaeologus, the Greek emperor who had founded the kingdom of Euboea, re-established a Byzantine empire, but more as a memory of the past than as a force of the present.

The middle-eastern arena turned in those years into a simmering cockpit of peoples at war with one another. The Turks and the Mongol hordes had already made their appearance and would dominate the scene for centuries to come, wiping out the ephemeral reconstitution of an empire that endured as long as it did only because of the divisions and the balance of enemy forces.

The fall of Constantinople was judged to be imminent, but it was delayed by at least 50 years by the presence of the Mongol troops of Tamerlane, who in their turn harried the Turks. In this way a precarious equilibrium was established in the East and Venice turned more of her attention towards Italian matters. The beginning of the 15th century saw the start of a new political phase defined in the expression "Venice turns towards the Mainland". Several factors combined to bring about this political volte-face: the need to have "the back protected" in a changing situation, the need to control routes of communication and the usefulness from an economic point of view of territorial expansion. In the Italian arena several small powers coexisted in a constant but precarious balance. Venice made her move quickly before anything could change this balance to her disadvantage.

Venice, besides, required a hinterland for many of her necessities: supplies of food including fresh water, timber, the use of alternative roads across the Alps should those of Lombardy be closed to her, as well as the obvious requirement of not having neighbours right on the borders of the lagoon. Nor could the immediate utility of the conquest of a vast agricultural territory have escaped the "fathers" of the Republic. One of the first acts after the occupation of the Mainland was in fact the appropriation of part of the demesne, i.e. the undivided public patrimony of the city, which was then sold to Venetian patricians. Thus in times when the "Stato de mar" was causing so much anxiety, the city sought to create a long-lasting alternative, in case of the loss of possessions in the East and to create an opportunity for the integration of commercial profits through investment in property.

Antonio Vasillacchi known as Aliense, Disembarkation at Venice of Caterina Cornaro Queen of Cyprus, detail. Museo Correr.

In 300 years, then, Venice had succeeded in acquiring both a "Stato de mar" and one on the mainland; the first, the "sea state", in order to facilitate her own trade to the maximum and the second, land-based, to create a hinterland as a back-up to this, and to make her presence felt on the Italian scene. Despite her uneven success and the loss of territories, the Republic had succeeded in remaining one of the greatest powers of the time. At the end of this period, however, her overall strength was severely tested, with Venice finding difficulty in holding on two fronts, and being forced to start giving way in the East. After 1500 she began her long, but final decline. It was, in any case, the development of trade, the true supporting structure of the Venetian economy, that provided the greatest impetus for her growth over these three centuries. This was helped by the improvement in techniques of navigation and shipbuilding as well. Towards the end of the 13th century mariners had at their disposal the *portolano*, an early and primitive chart drawn to scale that permitted the identification of coastlines, the location of ports and the calculation of the distance of each of these from the next. A further technical innovation consisted in the attachment of a magnetic needle to the card showing the direction of the winds which, rotating freely on a pivot, formed a rudimentary compass. The relative security provided by these aids permitted a greater freedom of navigation and of route. It was no longer necessary to heave to at night off the coast and voyages could be made even in the more meteorologically unfavourable seasons. At the same time techniques of construction were settling down into two types of sailing ship:

A. Piazza, The Departure of Francesco Morosini for the Levant, detail. Museo Correr.

the galley, long and narrow, and the *cocca*, of a roundish shape. The galley was much more manoeuvrable and was the typical boat used for combat. A "merchant galley" existed, however, for the transport of goods with soldiers on board. But the tonnage of the galleys was always limited, although from the 13th century on ships of 200-250 tons were built and, towards the end of the 15th century, as much as 400-500 tons. More suitable for the transport of goods, especially if they were bulky ones like cotton, was the *cocca*, which could be as large as 500-600 tons (Genoa built one of 1000 tons at the end of the 14th century) but was much less manoeuvrable and slower. Above all the *cocche* were unsuitable for combat and had to be escorted on long passages.

Galleys were used as merchant ships when it was necessary for them to be ready for combat at the same time. They carried a mixed crew of sailors, oarsmen and armed soldiers. When it came to a fight the latter could count on the help of the oarsmen whose work was essential only for the manoeuvres of leaving and entering port and when the ship was becalmed. Shipbuilding soon became a kind of state industry. The Venetian government had decided to concentrate the public shipyards in the area to the east of the city, towards the port of the Lido, which soon became known as the Arsenal. There are records of the Arsenal dating back to 1104. It was subsequently expanded and at the height of its activity employed 4,000-5,000 skilled workers, especially *marangoni* (carpenters) and caulkers.

A visit to the Arsenal was obligatory for any foreigner who wished to discover the secret of Venice's strength. Admiring travellers have left extravagant descriptions in their memoirs of the huge size of the place, of the number of ships under construction and of the skill and speed of the workers. The construction of ships required a constant supply of enormous quantities of timber, which had to be brought in from the hinterland, from Bellunese and Friuli. This demand, in addition to that for tree-trunks suitable for the construction of foundations, required labour for felling and for transport.

The deforestation of vast areas, especially in the mountainous zone of Venetia, is a not inconsiderable cause of the permanent hydrogeological problems of the region.

Small private boat-houses sprung up alongside the Arsenal for smaller-sized ships suitable for the transport of goods either by river or on voyages to Istria and Apulia. After 1324 the *mude* – as these voyages in convoy were called – were regular events and up until the 16th century were made almost every year in spring and summer except in the event of major war. The principal destinations were Romania, which meant Constantinople in practice, Beirut, Alexandria in Egypt and the Barbary coast, but also Flanders, especially after 1385, Aigues Mortes, London, Bruges, Valencia and Southampton.

From the 14th century on the nobles were in a majority and played an active part in trade, sailing and handling affairs directly in Constantinople as well as in Egypt, Syria and

Antonio di Natale, Plan of the Arsenal. Museo Correr.

View of a boat yard.

Flanders. Very often a family maintained its own commercial bases in a warehouse. Here a member of the family superintended acquisitions inside the region and distributed the merchandise that arrived from the metropolis, with a close exchange of information with the "management of the firm", run from Venice by the father or elder brother. At the same time as its expansion, the stakes in the balance of trade altered from the 13th century on. Until then the Venetian merchants had carried raw materials (wood, iron, wool) to the Orient and returned with spices and perfumes, but also with textile goods. The superiority of the Orient in this field began to wane from around 1200-1300, an undoubted sign of the progress made, not only in technology field but also in organization, by Italian and European manufacturers. Woollen cloth was especially easy to sell on the eastern markets. The convoys from Flanders brought it to Venice in growing quantities for distribution in Romania, Egypt and Syria, where it was exchanged for spices, cotton and dyes which made the same journey in reverse.

It seems certain, however, that the balance of trade with the East showed a quite substantial deficit for long periods, and this had to be overcome by the export of precious metals and of gold and silver coins.

Venice very soon developed a single centre for business. Just as the Square represented the stage and seat of political and religious power, Rialto established itself from the 12th century onwards as the place where the transactions and kindred activities of commerce took place. Thus Rialto always represented a privileged viewpoint for the monitoring of the economic trends: the level of trade in any pe-

G.B. Brustolon, The Church of San Giacometo and the Rialto Market.

riods was revealed by the fervour of the activity to be seen there. In 1172 the bank on the side of San Marco was linked to the market by a bridge of boats. In 1181 this link was made permanent by the construction of a wooden bridge. The market on Rialto was to establish itself as a kind of permanent trade fair, where dealing took place in the spices and other goods that arrived in Venice from the East and the West on prearranged dates and where merchants came from all over Europe not just to do business but also attracted to the unique economic observatory that it had become. Under the porticos of the small square of San Giacomo, one of the oldest Byzantinian churches in Venice, were set up the *banchi di scrittura*, the privately run banks of the period, where merchants held in deposit the sums necessary to their trade and which were transferred from one account to another simply against the signature of the depositor. The bankers carried out complex operations of exchange between different currencies as well, on payment of a small commission. So circulation through the banking system took its place alongside that of the currency, resumed vigorously after 1202 with the issue of the silver gross. In the more immediate vicinity of San Giacomo were to be found the shops for more costly merchandise. Less valuable or more cumbersome goods were traded on the banks of the canal, to facilitate loading and unloading; the two banks on each side of the bridge are still called today the bank of Wine and the bank of Coal. Beyond the bridge were the oil depositories – on the present-day riva dell'Ogio (bank of Oil) – and the food market. Numerous public offices were built on Rialto which were concerned with the regulation of the market and of taxes.

Libro Primo. 121

Ne Campi, & luoghi publici della Città di Venetia ritrouansi alcuni huomini chiamati Facchini, i quali per guadagno portano merci, massarie, & robbe da un luogo all'altro.

"huomini chiamati Facchini" (men called Dockers), from C. Vecellio, Habiti antichi et moderni di tutto il mondo, Venice 1590.

San Giacomo dell'Orio, the church seen from the campanile.

Fondaco dei Tedeschi.

Many buildings connected with commercial functions went up near the bridge. Of primary importance was the "Fontego dei Tedeschi", established in 1225 and rebuilt several times before attaining its present form in 1508. An important community was the Jewish one, at first concentrated on Giudecca then at Marghera on the mainland and finally at Cannaregio in the famous ghetto that still exists today. Here an exceptional density of population was attained, 5,000 inhabitants packed into multi-storey constructions set in a small area that also housed essential services.

All dealings between West and East had to be in the hands of Venetian merchants and only these were allowed to convey goods overseas, on Venetian ships. Venice remained faithful to this creed until the late 17th century, when the decline of her function as an intermediary became evident. Obviously the taxes on trade were among the biggest sources of revenue for the state. Customs dues were levied on all goods imported and exported: the duty payable to the Treasury was set at one fortieth of their value for foreign merchants and one eightieth for Venetians.

The end of the 13th century saw the conclusion of the process that had brought the relatively narrow circle of the nobility to the top in the Republic, where all power was concentrated in their hands. Venice has quite rightly gone down in history as an oligarchic republic with a caste that enjoyed and monopolized political rights in opposition to the other orders. The formal sanction to the dominance of the nobles came in 1297 with the move known as the "lock-

Aerial view with the Campo del Ghetto (The square of the Ghetto).

ing of the Great Council". After this date the only people admitted to the highest government assembly were those who had belonged to it over the previous four years or who were co-opted by means of a special procedure. But the oligarchic monopoly of the heights of power in the state had begun long before. It has been shown how right from its remote origins there was a clear class division among the inhabitants of the Rialto group of islands and how it was only within the stratum of the *maiores* that the uprisings took place that would bring a group, often bloodily, to the positions of command.

The Quarantia – so-called because it was initially made up of forty members –, was formed in 1180 with jurisdiction over financial matters, monetary control and judicial affairs. It was slowly deprived of authority by the council of the "Pregàdi", or the "Requested" – so-called because messengers were dispatched to request its members to attend meetings – set up in 1230 and destined to become the body where magistrates from several different sectors gathered to form a genuine collegial organ of government. In 1310 appeared the Council of Ten which, apart from exercising wide investigative powers, partly through the examination of secret denunciations collected at various points in the city, took on exceptional importance over the course of the 16th century. It was responsible for handling all the major and most delicate political affairs, whether internal or external.

It is very difficult to establish a precise line of demarcation between the jurisdictions of each organ of government: the Great Council, the Signoria – made up of the Doge, the six councillors and the three leaders of the Quarantia whose

G. Zampini, The Glass Vendor, 17th-century print. Museo Correr.

G. Bella, Hall of the Council of Ten. Galleria Querini Stampalia.

place was subsequently taken by the three leaders of the
Ten –, the Quarantia, the Senate and the Council of Ten
cannot be fitted into the pattern of the threefold division of
power – legislative, administrative and judicial – that is
proper to the modern theory of political science.

The uncertainty over the spheres of competence of the
Councils, however, emphasized the collective exercise of
power, above all amongst those who belonged to the nar-
rowest and most influential circle. The dynamics of decision, the slow passing of files from office to office and the
very opposition between different organs over the same
matter permitted the development of a lengthy mediation
that took into account the different positions and went further than a sterile argument over the jurisdiction of individual magistratures. Power, in short, was wielded, both
inside and outside the collegial bodies, by the richest and
hence most influential families. The patritiate very soon
split into those who, coming from the strongest classes,
carried out commercial activities in their youth and returned home at the age of around 40-45 to take over the
handling of affairs of state, and the poor patricians whose
chief means of support were the meagre returns to be

*Bailo, from the "Codex
Grevembroch". Museo
Correr.*

Jacopo de' Barbari,
Perspective Plan of Venice,
detail with the Rialto bridge
area. Museo Correr.

drawn from the second rate magistracies, along with marginal financial and commercial operations. Between 1200 and 1500 this growth was enormous; it may be said, looking at the extraordinary picture left us by Jacopo de' Barbari – dated 1500 in fact – that the city was already very similar in appearance to what it is today.

From the 13th century – a time when wooden houses were still predominant – onwards a massive work of construction had begun.

Three strongly characterized zones stand out clearly from de' Barbari's plan: the square, the Arsenal and the most important residential zone, consisting of the buildings facing onto the Grand Canal from the area of the Rialto Bridge – still built out of wood – to the Basin.

The canal marked the boundary of what might be called the city centre, where the wealthiest noble families were installed.

Erected around 1749 by the
architect Lorenzo Boschetti,
the façade of San Barnaba is
of the classical lean-to type,
with a triangular tympanum
and half-columns with
Corinthian capitals.

There was no precise functional zoning of the remaining part, where housing and commercial and industrial activities existed side by side. But the continuity of the built-up area was often interrupted by *campi*, which usually stretched in front of the parish churches and were used as a public space dedicated to community activities, both civil and religious.

In some places housing for homogeneous groups of residents was concentrated. In the parish of San Barnaba, behind the Academy, were to be found the poor nobles, who were in fact known as "Barnabotti". In the areas lying in front of the Arsenal, on the shore of the lagoon, three groups of terraced houses, called the "Marinarezza" can be seen on the plan. Still standing today, these were the first

Santi Giovanni e Paolo.
The apses, with their many
openings, alternate
mullioned windows with two
lights set above one another
with circular apertures.

The main façade, final stage
in the 14th-century
reconstruction of the Frari,
dominates the scene of the
square by its monumentality.

large-scale form of working-class building which the Republic had put up for sailors. The poorer classes were located in more outlying districts, in the areas of Cannaregio and Dorsoduro, in overcrowded and very wretched housing still largely built out of wood, or they occupied the mezzanine and top floors of grander and richer houses.

The plan also shows the two large Gothic churches, on an extremely unusual scale for the urban landscape of the day, of Santi Giovanni e Paolo and of the Frari, with their attached convents. The former was erected by the Dominicans and was begun in 1246, but not consecrated until 1430. The latter was built by the Franciscans between 1430 and 1443. The churches are an example of the positive results that could be produced by the rivalry between two religious orders. The eastern part of the city was dominated by the area of the Arsenal, which included a large basin, numerous covered slipways and, on the south side, the auxiliary buildings of the rope factories and the workshop for the manufacture of oars.

Between the Arsenal and the square lay the harbour zone; closer to the Piazzetta for the passenger traffic, more towards the Arsenal for goods traffic. Here the ships were moored. Goods were transhipped from them onto lighters which carried them either to the warehouses of Rialto where the boats stopped only long enough to load and unload, given the lack of space and the large number of boats in constant arrival, or to private depots. Other ships

Canaletto, the Customs point and the bank of the Zattere on the Giudecca Canal, detail. Milan, Crespi collection.

moored in front of San Marco, behind the Customs point, for the transfer of salt to the appropriate storehouses if necessary, or docked on the shore in front where the granaries stood in the space now occupied by the royal gardens.

Activity must have always been intense, then, in the whole of the basin, which has consistently been represented in paintings and prints as full of movement and colour. It must have been especially lively and chaotic during the period of the year when the rich *mude* left on or returned from their voyages to the East and West. Moreover, the square was for centuries the only real gate of entry to the city. Venice was not linked to the mainland until the middle of the last century. Anyone arriving there at an earlier date must necessarily have landed here, whether he came from the port of the Lido, by sea, or followed the Brenta and the arm of the lagoon that joined up with the wide canal of Giudecca. A number of important alterations were made to the basilica of St. Mark.

The new higher and more slender cupolas, which gave the building a more soaring and less oriental appearance, were added in the 13th century. Work on the Gothic decoration of the facade was carried out between 1385 and 1415. It was largely these alterations that gave the basilica the appearance it has today. Inside the church, alongside the older mosaics of the atrium with their more uniform style, new mosaic pictures on different lines appeared, on whose car-

On the following page
Michele Giambono, Birth of the Virgin, mosaic. Saint Mark's, Mascoli Chapel.

toons great painters of every period had worked. Together with the multicoloured marbles these mosaics created astonishing effects, with the light reflected and filtered by the five Byzantine semicylindrical cupolas.

The rebuilding of the Palace, which had begun in 1340 as well, was completed in 1550, although two disastrous fires in 1574 and 1577 made it necessary to reconstruct the wings facing the canal and basin. In place of the previous construction, with its two lateral towers, the present-day building was taking shape, beginning with the sides facing the wharf. This was the site of the hall for meetings of the Great Council, by this time very large: the old seat of the assembly on the ground floor must have been inadequate by then.

This section, which was begun in 1340 and completed in 1365, and embellished by large central windows in 1404 to a design by Pier Paolo delle Masegne, determined the choice of style and external appearance for the wing at right-angles to it.

Begun in 1422, this had to join up with the Porta della Carta, the triumphal and monumental entrance to the Palace designed in a flowery Gothic style by Giovanni and Bartolomeo Bon. The entrance leads to the Stair of the Giants which Andrea Rizzo completed in 1501 and which takes its name from the large statues of *Neptune* and *Mars* placed there by Sansovino in 1554. The Palace was built by more than one hand and over successive periods, but the result was a collective work of singular stylistic continuity. The principle characteristic of the building lies in its inversion of the relationship of mass; the massive upper part in fact, although lightened by the pattern of rose-coloured lozeng-

Saint Mark's. The lunette of the portal of Sant'Alipio with the Translation of the Body of Saint Mark (ca. 1260). On the right, general view toward the presbytery. The walls are faced with slabs of precious marble.

Gentile Bellini, Portrait of Doge Giovanni Mocenigo. Museo Correr.

Ca' d'Oro, the cord-shaped decoration of the corner, detail.

es and broken in its rhythm by the large windows and the grandiose Gothic balcony, stands on the loggia of sharply curved arches, which in its turn stands on the Gothic arcade of low columns. On the capitals of the arcade, taking a decorative motif from the grandiose portals of French cathedrals, precious sculptures represent multiple motifs in groups such as the signs of the zodiac, the vices and the cardinal virtues, the ages of man, the seasons and the human races. Many of the architectonic and stylistic features of the Palace became dominant elements in the architecture of houses as well. The Gothic arrived late in Venice and was assimilated and developed there in a wholly characteristic manner, turning into the most flowery of forms, above all in private buildings made up of 3 or 4 storeys, depending on whether there was only one *piano nobile* or two.

A dominant element in the evolution of the style was the arch: the series of small indigenous round arches in the loggias of the Veneto-Byzantine period was replaced by lancet arches, which often had a small point at the top, suggesting the influence of Moorish forms. This is also hinted at by the horseshoe arches, which were much less common. A further development of the lancet arch, especially from the 15th century onwards, was the trilobate arch, with the insertion of three small arches, two at the sides and one in the centre. The central part of the *piano nobile* of the houses was traversed by rows of windows, a typical example is the Ca' d'Oro, where the florid Gothic is by now completely dominant. Another very common and characteristic element to be found in the Doges' Palace is the cor-

Ca' d'Oro, façade.

ner coping, with its twisted spiral decoration that recalls the ropes of a boat and which is used to break up the continuity between adjoining facades of the Palace, as well as on the doorways and as frame for the windows.

There was also a flurry of activity in the construction of churches and monasteries. These last were for the most part sited on the islands scattered over the lagoon, forming an urban continuum whose sense has now been lost.

This fervent building and artistic activity saw the collaboration of architects, painters, artists and craftsmen from outside the city. Venice became a cross-roads where the cultural ferments of the Italian mainland and the ultramontane territories were superimposed on the now exhausted ones of Byzantine art and culture.

Gentile da Fabriano was called on to paint in the Hall of the Great Council in 1408, Paolo Uccello worked on the cartoons for the new mosaics in San Marco in 1425 and Andrea del Castagno in the apse of the church of San Zaccaria in 1442. Except for Masaccio and Fra Angelico, all the greatest Tuscan masters spent a period of their life in the lagoon city. Between 1474 and 1475 Antonello da Messina stayed in Venice and his work left its mark on the greatest painters then active in Venice. Among them stand out the members of two indigenous families: the Vivarini and the Bellini. In the numerous polyptyches by Antonio Vivarini, who worked with his brother Bartolomeo and son Alvise, iconic forms of distant Byzantine ancestry persist alongside a more marked concern with form, under the influence of the Tuscans, while remaining within the ambit of a late Gothic formulation. Jacopo Bellini belongs within this cat-

Andrea del Castagno, Saint Luke, detail of the cycle of frescoes depicting the Eternal Father with the Four Evangelists and Saints (1442). San Zaccaria.

San Zaccaria, façade.

Vittore Carpaccio, Saint Jerome leading the Lion to the Monastery, detail. Scuola di San Giorgio degli Schiavoni.

Vittore Carpaccio, Dream of Saint Ursula. Gallerie dell'Accademia.

egory too, but his sons moved away from it. Giovanni in particular attained, over the long period of his activity, to a maturity of expression, in part the result of a more rapid assimilation of other schools, which made him one of the greatest artists of his age. His brother Gentile, on the other hand, was to serve as a model for later scene-painters, especially with his famous *Procession to San Marco* of 1496 – a historical document of great value for the detailed description of the square that it has given us. Another painter of scenes was Carpaccio who has left us an evocative view of the Rialto Bridge at the end of the 15th century. His work was marked by a more intense chromatism with hints of the fantastic, and was rich in oriental influences especially in his scenes from the life of St. Ursula and in the canvases for the Scuola di San Giorgio degli Schiavoni. Among the most important architects of the Quattrocento were Pietro Lombardo and above all, Mauro Coducci. The name of the former, a sculptor as well, is linked to the Church of Santa Maria dei Miracoli of clearly Renaissance stamp. He is known in particular, for having propagated Tuscan culture in Venice. The latter played a primary rôle in the renewal of Venetian architecture in a Renaissance sense in the church of San Michele in Isola, in the facade of San Zaccaria, in the churches of San Giovanni Crisostomo and Santa Maria Formosa and in the reconstruction of the Scuola di San Giovanni Evangelista. He also designed the new building of the Procuracies, adjacent to the Clock Tower that he had built as well. Coducci left a very lofty example of assimilation of the new style to the surrounding environment in the facade of Ca' Vendramin-Calergi –

which now houses the Municipal Casino. The majestic classicism of this building was to give a lead to the architecture of the whole of the 16th century. Public works were undertaken extensively as well both for the consolidation of the physical structure of the city and for the reclamation of marginal areas for its expansion. A network of bridges became necessary to ensure rapid connections. Bridges without parapets were built out of stone to replace the rudimentary footbridges.

Philippe de Commynes, the globe-trotting French ambassador, preserved in his memoirs an unforgettable record of the lagoon city at the end of the 15th century: "My wonder was great on seeing the position of that city and seeing so many bell towers and monasteries and large buildings all on the water and the people with no other way of getting about than in those boats, of which I believe they could muster at least thirty thousand but which are very small. Around the city, in the space of less than half a French league, there are at least seventy monasteries for men and women all on islands, very beautiful and rich in buildings and ornaments and fine gardens. And this is not counting those of the four mendicant orders that are inside the city, the seventy-two parish churches and many confraternities; and it is a very strange thing to see such grand and beautiful churches built on the sea [...] They took me along the main street, which they call the Grand Canal and is very wide. The galleys pass down the middle and I saw ships of four hundred tons and over near to the houses, I think it to be the most beautiful street in the whole world and the most well constructed, and it crosses the entire city".

Vittore Carpaccio, Two Venetian Noble Women. Museo Correr.

Canaletto, A Race on the Grand Canal. Woburn Abbey, Duke of Bedford collection.

The decline

The Republic's loss of influence was more clearly demonstrated by her secondary rôle in European affairs. If Venice followed a policy of neutrality, that looked to France in so far as she was anti-Spanish and anti-Habsburg, this was more and more out of necessity rather than choice.

This was clearly recognized by the European states, so that even the political rôle of a balance which Venice still had at the beginning of the 16th century was reduced: diplomatic action that was not backed up by economic and political power had by now only a marginal influence. Hence the political and economic decline of Venice was drawn out over a long period that stretched from the beginning of the 16th century to the first decades of the 17th. Significant foreshadowings of this, however, can be made out as early as the 15th century. This long and slow decline was brought about by a combination of negative factors, which pushed the Serenissima into an eccentric position with respect to the "new world", and positive factors that braked her fall and mitigated the disruptive effects of the new international situation. The first of these was, of course, the rise of the national states of the great powers, with their powerful armies and much more extensive possessions than the north-east part of Italy under the rule of the "Dominante", and the second was the geographic discoveries that made the world a much vaster place and produced lasting and disruptive effects on trade and its routes.

Even in the 15th century knowledge of the world had been greatly expanded. It was in fact in Venice, between 1450 and 1459, that a friar, Fra Mauro, on the island of San Michele had made one of the most famous maps of the world. It was the result of patient work by a team that had collected material through reports of voyages and explorations of new regions, combined with fascinating hypotheses such as that of the possibility of circumnavigating Africa.

Navigation at sea was, even then, much less approximate than it had been two centuries earlier. The use of the compass and the consultation of *portolani* were by this time widespread. On the other hand the complex trigonometrical calculations that permitted the determination of distances by reference to the stars had been, worked out theoretically, but were as yet very rarely applied.

However the geographical discoveries – and this is particularly evident in the voyage of Christopher Columbus – were to a large extent empirical and preceded the time when the use of astronomical navigation became fully established. The navigators worked on the basis of very vague hypotheses, it was knowledge that progressed on the basis of the first-hand experience of sailors and not the other way round. The use of new types of boats helped to speed up these discoveries: the highly celebrated caravelles, for instance, with their reinforced sails; these used a square sail for propulsion and a lateen sail for steering, and had an elongated hull and low tonnage.

However they soon turned out to be inadequate for the

Side page
Jacopo Tintoretto, Finding of the body of Saint Mark, detail. Milan, Pinacoteca di Brera.

Ship presented to doge Francesco Mocenigo, from V. Coronelli, "Navi o vascelli, galee, galeazze, galeoni e galeotte... raccolte nell'Accademia degli Argonauti, dedicate all'Illustrissimo et... don Nicola Ghizzi...", Venice 1692.

Jacopo Palma the Younger, Portrait of the Doge's Wife Morosina Morosini Grimani. Museo Correr.

transport of precious cargoes of gold and silver from the rich mines of the Americas. For these voyages they were replaced by large galleys – the fabled galleons – with 3 or 4 masts and a respectable tonnage (300-400 tons), that were also capable of maintaining a fairly good cruising speed.

The carrying out of ocean voyages continued to improve knowledge of winds unknown to the peoples of the Mediterranean. Familiarity with these extremely useful means of propulsion allowed the development of long-range routes that had been dreaded up till that time. The countries which paid more attention than any others to the new opportunities were Spain and Portugal. The latter, on the threshold of the 16th century, had a population of no more than 800,000.

When, in 1620, the first ships arrived at the Venetian port carrying pepper, cinnamon and cloves from the West and no longer from the East, it began to sink in just how much the function of the Serenissima had changed.

Venice continued to handle trade with the Orient on a more modest level, dealing in other products: cotton, sugar linen, wax, hides and wool from the Balkans. With the loss of Candia (Crete) in a war that had swallowed up vast resources and that had appeared ill-fated from the first, the island's rich yields of oil and wine were lost as well. For trade with the West the port of Venice gradually became a regional port, whose sphere of territorial influence was limited to the imports and exports of her hinterland.

But the commercial policy of the Republic strenuously defended these two trends: on the one hand tax incentives to maintain the attraction of the port for the commercial and shipping organizations of Northern Europe, in competition above all with the Tyrrhenean ports; on the other the safeguarding of the shrunken Eastern trade with an obstinate defence, even by military means, of her own ships.

It was in fact the newly eccentric position of the traditional ports of the Mediterranean – from Constantinople to Alexandria in Egypt, from those of Dalmatia to those of Greece – and their resulting regional rôles that facilitated exchanges of raw materials and agricultural produce. Here, Venice had the advantage of an organization that derived from the assiduous work of many centuries. These were certainly very reduced rôles when compared with the past, but still economically significant and sufficient to ensure a flow of wealth, more modest though it may have been.

Quite a few of the Venetian patricians attributed the chief cause of the poor trade situation to the acquisition of rural estates on the Mainland. There were many who claimed that "neither carriages, nor horses, nor villas, nor perpetual leases had enriched Venice, but the trade in spices". In reality it is difficult with our present-day knowledge to give credit to the argument that it would have been enough to invest more resources in trade to have improved its fortunes, even though the land purchases formed an incitement to abandon risky maritime ventures. The Venetian patritiate of the Cinquecento was less inclined than its fathers to face the open sea and the hazards and privations of long voyages, but this was also because the prospects of gain were more uncertain. The negative effect of the immobilization of capital probably made itself felt in the second half of the 16th century, when the mercantile recovery could have absorbed more substantial investments. But money in any age, has never liked inactivity and would probably have found other channels for the earning of profits, without staying shut up in coffers. On the whole however, the investments in property by private individuals

Jacopo Tintoretto, Portrait of Doge Alvise Mocenigo. Doges' Palace.

Allegory of Commerce. Biblioteca del Museo Correr.

*Tintoretto, Procurator
Jacopo Soranzo. Gallerie
dell'Accademia.*

*Sala del Collegio, in Giacomo
Franco, "Habiti d'Homeni et
Donne venetiane...", Venice,
1610-14. Biblioteca Marciana.*

and the taxes confiscated by the state made the political domination of the mainland state a powerful brake on the economic decline of the "Dominante" and largely compensated the Republic for the vast sums she had spent on its defence in the second decade of the 16th century.

We have already seen how, during the 15th and the first few decades of the 16th centuries, a very much smaller group of nobles had established itself within the already restricted oligarchy, and was able to exercise, directly or indirectly, almost total control over the government. There is nothing surprising about this: it was the same Venetian system that created a very close tie between the political ruling class and trends in economic policy that answered to the interests of those who exercised political power. It should be understood that this did not necessarily mean that this more restricted group was a sort of lobby or clique. Rather it was a group of changing composition to which the most influential families of any one period belonged; this influence is understood to have very often been determined by the amount of property owned, especially if it had been owned over a long period.

Crises and financial upsets, such as those that occurred periodically as a result of the serious state of public finances – a typical example is the series of collapses in the first half of the 16th century of bankers and families compromised by the enormous sums owed to them by the Treasury – altered the composition of this power group.

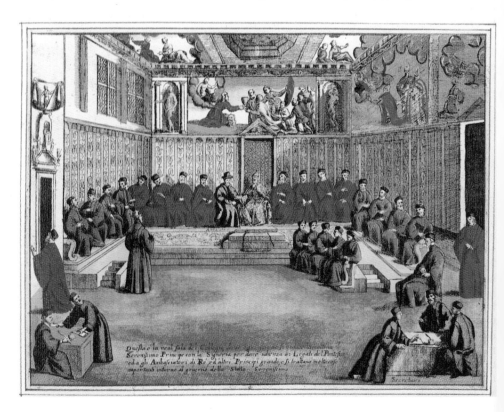

Tron houses, eighteenth century unking-class housing, facing the rio delle Terese.

The start of the 17th century saw, however, a further concentration of the reins of command, whose causes can be ascribed to the following: the shrinking in numbers of the nobility, the possibilities of amassing wealth from public positions and the concentration of wealth in forms that were less profitable but more secure investments and therefore less subject to swings of fortune.

Most significant of these was the decreasing demographic strength of the nobility, the result, as happens in all closed social organizations, of a gradual and irresistible fall in the birth rate. In 1581 the noble class numbered 6,068 and represented 4.5% of the population, 60 years later the number had fallen to 4,451, equal to 3.7% of the population. Although the two violent pestilences of 1575 and 1631 had struck the poor classes harder, this relative contraction continued inexorably. A hundred years later the nobles barely exceeded 3,000 in number and only represented a little over 2% of the resident population, a proportion which remained more or less constant. It should be realized, moreover, that between 1627 and 1798, 107 families formerly belonging to other social ranks were admitted to the nobility, a contribution of between 500 and 600 persons. Among these nobles, obviously only the adult males could be enrolled in the Great Council. And so there was a constant decrease in numbers with respect to the 2,500-3,000 registered in the 14th and 15th centuries, despite the lowering of the minimum age requirement to 18 – which became general after 1650 – and despite the additions, until the number fell below a thousand in 1769.

There were many noble lineages, therefore, that came to an end because of a lack of heirs. Apart from this process of natural selection, the concentration of power was favoured by the granting of public offices and future entry to the Great Council on the payment of a sum of money. It is obvious that the more powerful and wealthy families obtained more representation and more positions of command as a result of their financial resources. By now money played an ever more open part in admittance to elected office as well. Even the election of the doge was often organized

Banquet in the house of Nani Mocenigo in Venice, 1735. Museo Correr.

Rialto Bridge.

Ca' Corner, façade.

through parties who bought up the votes of the poorer patricians, manipulating the complex procedural mechanisms.

Moreover the very nature of the Magistratures had been perverted with respect to the reliable mechanisms of previous centuries, in which there must at least have been a very broad consensus. The shrinking of the patritiate itself exaggerated the process of delegation which gave, as we have seen, power to restricted groups in the different magistratures: to the inquisitors over the Council of Ten itself, to the leaders of the Forty, and to the Wise Men. Exceptions to the *contumacia* – when immediate re-election to a previously occupied post was forbidden – and to incompatibility were numerous, while the succession of a few powerful men to the key posts of government became more blatant. As the politics of the state as a whole changed, so did the course of the economy. Privileges were no longer granted to the merchants but with the attractive sharing out of the public domain, to those who invested on the mainland and those who purchased state bonds.

At this point the oligarchic closure that had begun three centuries before proved itself to be irreversible. With the changed conditions and the weakening of the oligarchy to the point that the driving force of the merchant patrician disappeared, no social group was in a position to get economic and political growth started again on different foundations. The class of "original citizens", which also possessed considerable financial means in its upper strata, was closely linked to the nobles, until it was tardily and uselessly incorporated, going along with and amplifying these choices. Hence the lack of any social dialectics guaranteed the oligarchy's retention of power, but on a narrower base. It is here then, in its total impermeability to the classes excluded from command, that the first clue to the decline of the Venetian pattern of growth is to be found: its concrete inability to evolve towards other types of social structure. The decline was halted, as we have seen, through the mobilisation of resources to the maximum and the strengthening of a restricted élite; a process which brought with it changes in the economic fabric and the growth of parasitical revenue – raising activities. Venice met the challenges of the new world, the geographic discoveries and the opportunities offered by technical innovations with the maintenance of her immobile structure. Her defeat was postponed in time by the favourable external conditions provided by a balance of the forces in the field, and of course by the skill of her diplomacy too along with what remained of the "culture of government" that derived from her intense past history. But it was the passing of time that would make her fall inevitable, widening the gap between the whirlwind of new doctrines and new forms of government and her own static fidelity to the past. The changes that were made to the urban fabric of Venice during the 16th century were no longer concerned with the overall layout of the city, firmly established since the end of the previous century. Rather they were internal changes: new buildings went up alongside old ones; existing architectural structures were altered and embellished, especially those of public buildings used for government functions. The Arsenal was the subject of intense work in the 16th century and in 1592 the Rialto Bridge was rebuilt in its present form. Above all, however, it was the transformation of the square by Sansovino, in the style that has been aptly named "State art", that gave shape to the self-glorification of the Serenissima. This was based on a rediscovery and reforging of the now long forgotten link with Roman culture.

Sansovino was the interpreter of this conception. Appointed curator in 1529, i.e. superintendent of the buildings of the square, he transformed it completely. Between 1529 and 1538 he completed the Old Procuracies, to a design by Coducci, so that they joined up with the Church of San Geminiano. Now vanished, this used to stand opposite the Basilica and Sansovino himself had rebuilt its facade in 1557. His plan for the construction of the new mint was accepted in 1536, and the building was finished in two stages. In 1537 work was begun on the Loggetta of the Campanile and in the same year he set about construction of the Library. This would be completed under the direction of Scamozzi, who took over from Sansovino after his death and who would also be in charge of building the New Procuracies. It is now possible to look at the square and perceive the stratification in time of its buildings, each of which is

Jacopo Sansovino, The Mint (La Zecca).

The Procuratie Vecchie.

*Libreria Marciana from
the quay.*

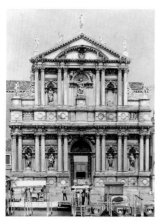

*Scalzi, façade. Typical
example of late Venetian
baroque (1672-1780).*

set in a different historical perspective, and at the same
time interpret its symbols of power. The New and Old
Procuracies are the wings and also the screen that closes
the square and their somewhat obsessive repetitiveness
sets off the Palace and the Church, which stand out as
clearly different.

The Library has a similar architectural style to the Procuracies, in which one sees the symbolical appearance of culture. Beside it stands the solid mint, symbol of economic
power, followed by the Granaries, symbol of abundance.
The Loggetta, sentry point to the Piazzetta, the wharf and
the entrance to the Palace, is at the same time a reference
to classicism and to the Roman spirit, bearing allegorical
decorations that serve to drive home this message. The
massive yet graceful profile of the Palace, which effective-
ly sums up all these symbolic functions in virtue of its more
distant presence on the scene, continues to dominate the
surrounding buildings. A sense of unity and ordered composition is created that is at once evident to anyone facing
the square from the basin.

Even the portico that runs along the whole southern part
as far as the Tower has a dual symbolic and practical signif-
icance, as a place of passage, meeting and popular partici-
pation. Above all this stands the Campanile, visible from
afar, but making it possible in turn to see into the distance,
an ideal observation tower overlooking the sea that played
such a large part in the economic, political and social life .

Santa Maria della Salute.

It is customary to place the construction of the church of La Salute (Health) – fruit of the votive offerings for liberation from the plague of 1630 – in the perspective of the scenographic interpretation of the city. In it a more spectacular relationship between the building and its environment is given emphasis, accentuating the monumental and celebratory character of the surrounding area. The architect of the plan for La Salute was Longhena, a pupil of Scamozz. While Longhena had absorbed the lessons of Sansovino and Palladio, he turned them into an example of the assimilation of the new baroque style. This is especially evident in the twin cupola, animated by the large volutes linking it with the tambour and by the contraposition of statues and obelisks. More properly baroque, on the other hand, are the facade and the interior of the church of the Scalzi that Longhena designed around 1660, and the church of the Ospedaletto. The baroque triumphed, in its more exaggeratedly decorative version, in the new facade of San Moisè as well, whose architect, Tremignon, collaborated with a Flemish sculptor, Arrigo Meyning.

Palazzo Barbaro (left) and Palazzo Dario.

Palladio too had worked in Venice, at the same time as Sansovino, but his work was certainly less appreciated, perhaps because he gave priority to the canons of his own artistic interpretation in his architecture. It would be ungenerous to suggest that Sansovino was more malleable to the demands and desires of the powerful of the time. If he was more in line with the conception of "State art", this

Il Redentore.

was not an opportunistic choice on his part, but a cultural one that came out of his own artistic maturity. It is no accident however that the finest examples of Palladian art in Venice, the church of Il Redentore and the church on the island of San Giorgio, are set outside the city proper. In these Palladio remains faithful to what critics call his anticlassical component, which they see above all in the "triumph of pure light over geometric space".

The greatest architects have also left significant marks on private buildings. Thus Sansovino's name was linked to Ca' Corner, the building of imposing bulk known in fact as Ca' Grande, and Longhena's to Ca' Rezzonico and Ca' Pesaro, in which a classical sturdiness dominates which results in their being considered among the finest examples of 17th-century secular architecture.

Scamozzi and Palladio, on the other hand have left a stronger mark on the construction of villas, which spread over the Venetian countryside with the massive return to land purchases that took place in the 16th century. It was Palladio above all who conceived, while remaining completely faithful to the canons of construction he expressed in his work *I quattro libri dell'architettura*, a form of villa that starts out from a dominant central body – pivot of social life, entertainment, banquets and festivities – linked through arcades to lateral rustic buildings, as if to underline the owner's control over agricultural activity. A perfectly successful example of this formulation is the Maser villa, in which Veronese worked.

For a considerable proportion of the Cinquecento Venice was considered the European capital of painting, and rightly so. This was encouraged by the greater number of patrons of the arts and religious orders to be found there and by the desire of the Republic to celebrate her own magnificence through illustrations of her present and past history and allegories of the city. It was above all for the frescoes of the Palace that the great artists of the century were called on, one by one: Giorgione, Titian, Tintoretto and Veronese. The majority of these works have been destroyed in subsequent fires, as were those by the Bellini and Carpaccio, who had worked there previously. Only a small number of works on canvas by these great painters are still in Venice, most of them having been dispersed throughout the galleries and museums of the world.

Even the frescoes which Giorgione had painted for the Fondaco dei Tedeschi have not survived. Giorgione had received the commission for the paintings of the Warehouse from the Great Council as a result both of the extensive fame that he already enjoyed and of the low price at which he offered his work to the Republic, following what was in fact a promotional policy.

He was in any case a man of wide cultural interests and strong artistic personality, dissatisfied with working in other people's studios even as a young man. In his painting he developed an accentuated glorification of the relationship between man and nature and a highly colourful description of the elements of landscape. These themes are recognizable in the *Three Philosophers*, in the *Sleeping Venus* and in the highly celebrated *Tempest* in the Academy.

Giorgione, The Storm, detail. Gallerie dell'Accademia.

Titian, Presentation of the Virgin in the Temple, detail. Gallerie dell'Accademia.

Titian, pala Pesaro, detail. Frari.

Jacopo Tintoretto, Last Supper. San Giorgio in Isola.

Lorenzo Lotto, Portrait of Laura da Pola. Milan, Pinacoteca di Brera.

Veronese, Triumph of Venice, detail. Doges' Palace.

Titian, who was born in the mountains, also set out to make himself known to and appreciated by the public commissioners, partly in order to make his way amidst the tremendous competition from so many established contemporary artists. His vast body of work, celebrated by critics of all ages, had an important part to play in the development of pictorial art in his century and was a sign of a more marked receptivity to the sumptuous chromatic forms that would dominate the painting of the Cinquecento. At the age of fifty, Titian came under the influence of the manneristic forms which were belatedly penetrating as far as Venice from Rome, Tuscany and Emilia. This helped to bring about changes in his design, in which chiaroscuro effects prevailed from that time on. Works by Titian that have remained in Venice are the scenes from the Bible in La Salute and the altarpieces of the Assunta and Pesaro ai Frari. Tintoretto was a more totally Venetian artist, by birth and by virtue of the fact that he stayed in his city of origin.

Of a later generation than Titian, he made use of manneristic themes right from the start, counterposing them by a style based on a rapid touch, almost sketching figures in contrast to the dense tonal texture of the older master.

His more important works – including the *Crucifixion* in the Scuola di San Marco, which he decorated with frescoes between 1564 and 1580, the *Paradise* and the *Capture of Zara* in the Doges' Palace – are choral masterpieces in which the crowd is the protagonist and moves amidst twinkling lights, lent rhythm by its very fluid design. In the *Last Supper* in San Giorgio Maggiore, on which he worked until shortly before his death, he took manneristic accents to a point where they shade into surrealism.

San Sebastiano, façade.

Jacopo Bassano, Adoration of the Shepherds, detail. Gallerie dell'Accademia.

Side page
Giandomenico Tiepolo, Mondo novo, detail. Ca' Rezzonico.

The work of Paolo Veronese, who made his debut before the age of thirty with the decoration of the entire church of San Sebastiano, was more closely tied to a search for intense chromatic tonalities, accompanied by a leaning towards portraiture. The two elements were fused in the grandiose scenographic layouts of the *Suppers*, the most famous of which is now in the Louvre, while the painting he did for the Domenicans of Santi Giovanni e Paolo is in the Academy. The opulence and wealth of the city found a refined interpreter in Veronese, above all in the allegorical celebrations for the Sala del Collegio in the Doges' Palace and in the *Triumph of Venice*, his last work. Other painters were at work in Venice during the 16th century. Among these the most important were Jacopo Bassano and his son Leandro, Sebastiano Del Piombo, Pordenone, Palma the Younger and Palma the Elder.

The presence of numerous artists, the free circulation of ideas made possible by a publishing industry of which few European cities could boast, the simultaneous presence of different ethnic groups and Venice's character as a frontier city, a crossroads for diverse peoples and cultures, made the city a lively setting throughout the Cinquecento. But this tended to die out in the Seicento and the city was not prepared for an open encounter with the new experiences of the Age of Enlightenment. If the 14th and 15th centuries can be considered the golden years of economic

Canaletto, The Return of the Bucintoro to the Basin on Ascension Day. (Formerly) Milan, Crespi collection.

F. Guardi, Foyer, detail. Ca' Rezzonico.

expansion and of the monopoly of trade on the routes to the Orient, the 16th century is the apogee of opulent life.

Even during the 18th century there was no lack of cultural ferment and the free circulation of ideas and information. A great number of "gazettes" emerged, periodicals of various kinds filled with news about national and foreign events. Venice remained one of the most important centres of information, as she continued to be the centre of a flourishing book-trade. But the ideas did not penetrate; they spread but did not sink in. They lost their innovatory impetus and were stripped of their disruptive content in a fixed and sclerotic society that watched the cultural movement that was overrunning and transforming Europe with a curious but at the same time cynical detachment. Evidence of some permanent vivacity of culture was provided by the presence of schools of painting, which harked back to the great times of the Cinquecento rather than to the previous century. Outstanding among his contemporaries was Giambattista Tiepolo, a Venetian painter born at the end of the 17th century. In the works of his most mature period he echoes those of Veronese, returning to the harmonious complexity of his patterns of composition and the luminous intensity of his combinations of colour, barely tempered by an unexpected lightening of colour into a soft and luminous range of tones. The scenes from the story of Anthony and Cleopatra in Palazzo Labia and the paintings on the ceilings of the Scuola dei Carmini and of the church of the Scalzi derive from this formulation. His sons Lorenzo and especially Giandomenico continued his work, but also reproduced their father's paintings in engravings. A painter who had a great influence on Tiepolo's work was Piazzetta, an exponent of the late baroque decorative current, which did not always produce worthy results. Canaletto on the other hand represented the highest expression of the scene-painting genre, which had been given a rigorous start in Venice by the Friulian painter Carlevarijs, mainly through the production of etchings. Canaletto's huge compositions, sparkling with brilliant colour, in which emphasis is placed on grand architecture and on the tiniest of figures alike, achieved immediate success and were highly valued on the commercial market as well. The high level of Canaletto's work was kept up by the Guardi brothers, especially the younger one, Francesco, who often added to the views that touch of the fantastic and capricious that gave them originality. Pietro Longhi, on the other hand, in his youth a modest illustrator of history and mythology, turned his hand to sketches of Venetian life, portraits with a highly observant spirit and an acute sense of irony. The work of Rosalba Carriera was highly appreciated by his contemporaries, especially his celebrated portraits in which he interpreted the ideals of elegance and graceful manners proper to his society with great artistic sensitivity. To meet the demands of a rich and ever more numerous clientèle, the painter set up his own workshop where he employed assistants which explains the uneven quality of his works.

The influence of Longhena remained dominant in 18th-century architecture. The late baroque was represented by the Ticinese architect Domenico Rossi who designed

Rosalba Carriera, Young Man of the Leblond Family. Gallerie dell'Accademia.

I Gesuati, the façade and overall view of the interior.

The French in Venice,
engraving by Rouarge.
Biblioteca del Museo Correr.

Doge Ludovico Manin.
Doges' Palace.

the facade of the church of San Stae, the church of the Jesuits and the Palazzo Corner della Regina. But a return to Palladianism was already apparent in the facade of the Tolentini and the massive dimensions of San Simeon Piccolo, facing the present-day railway station. Massari too, in the facade of the Gesuati alle Zattere and in the Palazzo Grassi, took his inspiration from the Vicenzan architect in the ostentatious simplicity of the forms that he used. There was a return to Palladio's canons in the construction of country houses as well. The liberal flourishing of the arts, the architectural zeal for the embellishment and more often for the aggrandisement of what came from the past, the functional transformation of the city by wider bridges and paved streets in place of muddy alleys, and the way that daily life was characterized by less involvement and by a growing detachment from public posts even among the narrow circles of the patritiate ill concealed the anxiety and the strain of the imminent end.

When Napoleon fell on Milan in order to drive out the Austrians and pursued them through Venetian territory, Venice could do nothing to oppose the force of an army that within a brief period had occupied many cities of the mainland. Here belatedly echoing the magic words of the now triumphant revolutionary slogan, the local élites revenged themselves by forming governments hostile to Venice. Venetian ambassadors followed Napoleon's movements, careful to carry out his every desire, which became ever more burdensome. In the end he commanded the Venetian government to hand over power to a democratic municipal council: in practice he forced the dissolution of institutions

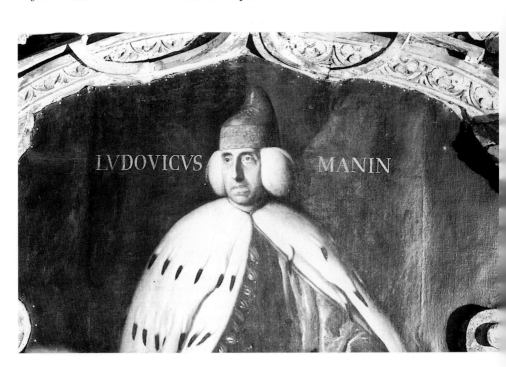

LVDOVICVS MANIN

*Conquest of Venice,
anonymous engraving.
Biblioteca del Museo Correr.*

with a thousand years of history behind them, accompany-
ing this order with an eloquent array of troops on the borders of the lagoon. On the 12th May 1797 Doge Lodovico
Manin made known Bonaparte's will to the Great Council,
accepting de facto the conditions imposed in order to "preserve unharmed the religion, the lives and the property of
all these greatly loved inhabitants". The attitude of the
Great Council was more cringing than submissive. Some
historian, a formalist beyond all reasonable limits, tells us
that this decision was taken in the absence of the legal quo-
ta of members. In reality the Republic's fate had been
sealed for some time, only wanting the last definitive push.
The desire not to lose the possessions on the mainland
played a part in this decision not to put up any resistance,
as the nobles feared their confiscation; but it was in any
case a forced choice. All the final acts of the drama are
marked by the fear and physical terror of a ruling class
that was by now irremediably outmoded. Thus the doge,
on learning on the 30th April of the billeting of enemy
troops Marghera, declared that one could not feel safe
even in one's own bed that night. When General Junot en-
tered the hall of the Great Council he found it hard, as he
himself relates, to suppress his laughter when he, the son
of a revolution that had changed the history of the world,
saw the doge and the Signoria dressed in their costumes
from another age and clearly showing their anxiety and
fear, making them a highly emblematic image of a ruling
class that had grown inept and cowardly. The parade of a
detachment of 4,000 French soldiers in St. Mark's Square,

The Scuola dei Luganegheri.

The railway station constructed during the Austrian period.

sent there to maintain order – an order which in any case no-one could have hoped to disturb – was the final image in the history of the *Repubblica Serenissima*.

But Venice did not die in 1797, even though traditional historiography would often like to see that year as a sharp and definitive, and irreparable caesura, between a before bound up with an irretrievable past and an after of abandonment, poverty and ruin. In any case, the end of Venice as a political entity left an indelible mark on the urban fabric. During the Napoleonic period demolition was begun. At times this was dictated by "health" requirements – this was the case with the Napoleonic gardens –, at others by the desire for self-glorification – for instance the gigantic statue erected to Napoleon in the Piazzetta and swept away with the second Austrian domination – and at yet others by the emergence of a different artistic taste, which showed little respect for the past – such as the demolition of the church of San Geminiano in the part of the square facing San Marco and its replacement by the Napoleonic Wing. It was the period of Austrian rule that had the greatest effect, with substantial modifications to the urban structure: the linking of Venice with the mainland by the railway bridge permanently altered her age-old relationship with the sea and extended the city towards its new land-based terminals.

Within the city itself a parallel project provided for an environment as little "different" as possible from "normal" cities. Hence more demolition was carried out to open up wide streets, especially in the "unhealthy" zones on the main traffic routes, and bridges were built at the Academy and at the Scalzi which increased the number of links between the two insular parts of the city, until then firmly

joined only at Rialto. One of the urban characteristics of Venice was slowly altered: the emergence of zones characterized by important economic functions dissolved the previous spread of functions and lack of zoning. In this way a "centre" was established, marked by the growing value of property, and a "periphery" where the emargination of the poorest groups was now more visible. Here a series of buildings providing working-class housing were taking shape. Especially during the first decades of the 20th century, the white-collar workers and middle-classes were housed in the intermediate zones, while the centre remained in the hands of the wealthy, creating the classic concentric hierarchy in direct proportion to the level of rent. Although the process of industrialization produced positive results, it also tended to turn Venice into a city with opportunities for growth like any other. Works and factories were expanded, as is demonstrated by the huge areas once occupied and now abandoned.

The prison.

Matters did not change substantially with Venice's entry into the Kingdom of Italy: the same paradigms maintained their validity. A new demolition plan was launched to make room for other wide *calli*, and attempts were kept up to increase the rôle of the port. These proceeded in fits and starts but did produce some positive and significant increases in activity. In 1880 the port was transferred to the end of the Giudecca canal, with the opening of the maritime station. It was above all here that connected activities were concentrated: it suffices to think of the construction over the next few years of the Stucky Mill, whose imposing outline determined and typified the profile of later constructions on the shore of the island of Giudecca, and of the numerous silos that now stand idle.

Stucky Mill, detail.

At the beginning of the 20th century a more comprehensive project for the zoning of different activities took shape. For industrial activities an external area, Marghera, was selected, in an area that had less planning constraints and environmental problems even though, as we now know, the effects have been the opposite of the objectives of that time. For the "bathing industry" the Lido was selected. These choices demonstrate how there had in the meantime been a rethinking of the search for a typology and a layout for the city that would assimilate it to the situation on the mainland. Already the idea was being put forward of emphasizing, instead, the city's difference and uniqueness. It was thought that it might have a rôle to play as the capital of European culture, as the initiatives of the Biennale would demonstrate.

Perhaps Venice had once again fallen prey to the poets of her myth. Just as in the 16th century she had decided on self-glorification, following in the wake of the many foreigners who had praised the peculiarities of the city, the celebrations of romantic literature curbed and conditioned the search for the negation of herself. In any case conservation and growth, the call of the new and attachment to the old, were already at the centre of her search for identity.

Venice, past and present

"Esto perpetua". Tradition has it that these were the last words which the dying Fra' Paolo Sarpi addressed to the Republic whose "reverent and ardent servant" he had declared himself to be.

"Be eternal": the augury was uttered at the height of the 17th century and referred to the political survival of the Serenissima and of her "singular government", to her by this time troubled and uncertain navigation between the great nation states that already dominated the European scene. Today the same wish is expressed for Venice as a city, for her unique forms, and for the heritage of art, history and culture that she contains, but in order to come true, this augury must be transformed into coherent action. The task is not an easy one and, in a sense, goes against history. In every civilization political and economic decline has unfailingly been accompanied by the decay of its monuments, that is of the images, the celebrations of itself that that civilization had produced; just as the urbanistic and architectural shell that accompanied this splendour also decays and is corrupted.

Ruskin, more than a century ago, had already taken this process for granted for the Queen of the Adriatic: "From the time when men affirmed their dominion over the sea, three states worthy of mention have emerged on its sands: Tyre, Venice and England. Of the first only the memory remains, of the second the ruins..." A law of nature that, according to the dictates of positivism, may be transferred to the study of societies: with the vital organs – trade – dead, everything goes to rack and ruin.

Then a new literary myth of the city was born, bound up with its situation apparently outside time, in a space and a setting so different that its form was no longer directly legible in its material connotations. Here then were the romantics, whom Venice "seduced and bewitched", here above all were the decadent poets of the dying city. During the 19th century the grave-diggers of the Serenissima filled thousands of pages on which they brought together "the echoes of activities and festivals with the dull sounds of marble breaking into pieces and falling into the water". The inhabitants are absent; they are not mentioned. At the most they are supernumeraries to a sealed fate, sharing the same destiny as the buildings in which they live, the wisest of them sunk in regret for the splendour of old. This aspect of the literary myth was the one that would last the longest, well beyond the century which generated it, and also become the most universally familiar.

The creation of this myth was to throw a veil over the real problems and their possible solutions and it has continued to feed on the past with little reference to the present.

And yet many things underwent changes in the 19th century. With the natural relationship between land and water inverted, the city was projected towards its terminals on land; broad *calli* permitted a reduction in pedestrian traffic unknown before that time and factories and workshops were set up to turn it into an atypical mainland city. Many

Side page
F. Guardi, The street of beggars looking toward the monastery of the Dominicans, detail. Bergamo, Accademia Carrara.

Pietro Longhi, The Dancing Lesson. Gallerie dell'Accademia.

Pietro Longhi, La Toilette. Gallerie dell'Accademia.

Canaletto, The Staircase of the Giants. Mexico City, Oberon de Paglie collection.

things also changed through decay, those irremediable consequences of the passing of time, which dimmed the intensity of the lively colours used by the great painters of the Cinquecento, dulled the sumptuous decorations of the interiors and crumbled the marble and stone of statues and buildings. Along with these came that decay that is just as hard to tackle, due to changes in the use of buildings, internal alterations and the multiplication of storeys in housing; changes which derived from the different living requirements once the city had ceased to play its social and economic rôle. And how can one forget the Napoleonic and Austrian plundering, a tribute perenially due as a result of the defeats at the hands of the city's new masters?

And on the other hand, how could it all have gone on as before? How is it possible, for instance, to maintain active and functioning – and therefore preserve in the most complete sense – more than a hundred churches for a population of 100,000? How to keep unaltered the interiors of the noble palaces on the Grand Canal without an élite with the means to make them into status symbols?

Hence it is useless to accuse an entire century of not hav-

ing adequately fulfilled its rôle of handing down to the next one, intact, the patrimony it inherited. The exigencies of life and the necessities of production and housing left their mark on the surrounding environment and on urban forms, superimposing their own memories on more remote ones. Moreover it should at least be acknowledged that new ways were being experimented with, tested and sought out at that time, even though the results were not always appreciable.

Despite all this (or perhaps as a result of all this?) Venice is not dead. Even to this day, the grave-diggers consummate their rites and continue to prophesy her imminent end. But is it enough to cross the city on a sunny day to squash these importunate and anxious nocturnal phantasms? The city bears the marks of decay, of the enormous problems imposed by the conservation of an artistic heritage concentrated in a restricted space. More mature however is the conviction that the survival of the city depends not only on the expert hands of the restorers and on the generosity of numerous foreign committees but also on the revitalization of the economy and on the consequent presence of different social strata capable of ensuring the continuity of the human environment, an environment that is so rich and stimulating in this city. So it may be said today that Venice can be saved if a balance is maintained between conservation and development, meaning by this a comprehensive policy that takes into account the physical environment of the lagoon and the hinterland that has gravitated around it. But it must be asked whether such an assertion, though important, is sufficient. Is it enough to say that two theories about Venice are juxtaposed, a conservationist one that would like the city to be turned into a place of meditation, of silence and of study, and a progres-

Ippolito Caffi, Venice, Snow and Fog. Ca' Pesaro.

Campo Santa Margherita in a nineteenth century photograph.

Rio del Pistor with its old houses.

sive one that wants it alive and kicking, with a complex economic and social fabric? Despite the fact that this overall plan is more clearly discernible today, although delicate in some of its parts, many difficulties stand in the way of its realization, as the last chapter of this book will attempt to explain. The bureaucratic sluggishness of intervention by the State, the speculative pressure of Italian and foreign capital, which would alter the structure of ownership of housing to the detriment of the residents, and the hypocritical opportunism of those who are in unanimous agreement over the "principles" but ignore them in everyday practice, these are all impending threats. Even in the exploitation of the city for tourism, which runs the risk of becoming its monoculture of production, there are inherent risks, as much on the side of demand as on that of supply, to use the cold language of the economists. In the use of the city as a tourist attraction do we not see an echo of the 19th-century myths of the "death of Venice" strengthened by a functional rhetoric based on the same myths?

Every literary image produces simplified stereotypes, just as every famous picture gives rise to a series of rough and inaccurate copies. Braudel says: "The unreal character of Venice is what creates its fascination and hoary myths, as of a world partly seen and partly dreamed, that we take into ourselves spontaneously. And that is just what is to be expected here. Each of us has his own way of loving this surprising city, different from that of the person standing next to him; each has his own way of making it part of himself at his leisure, of finding what he is seeking, whether it is the joy of living or even the contemplation of death. But it is always a question of a moment's rest or an alibi, or simply an interlude of a different sort of life".

In each of the ways in which the visitor confronts a city that is "unique in the world" there is to a lesser or greater extent, and more or less unconsciously, a bit of personally reworked stereotyping.

This is how the image of the Serenissima is broken up, fragmented into parts. There are the emblematic places, that are deputed to represent the whole; each of us has already seen and grown familiar with these places before seeing them in the flesh: the Square, the Grand Canal, the Rialto Bridge. For many visitors the tour of the city is limited to this obligatory itinerary. All the buildings that belong to the class of "monuments" – churches, palaces, museums – are visited as if they were detached from their urban context and from the history of which they are the product, as if they were churches, palaces, museums moved to some other part of the world. This is exacerbated by the necessity of (or the fashion for?) bringing together works of art in a restricted space, extracted from the place where they were born and where they often had a precise and definite relationship with the setting: in this way colours and tints are lost not only as a result of the marks left by time, but also because the intuition of the artist who had taken particular lighting conditions into account is broken.

Finally there is a large part of the city that acts as a back-cloth, that forms the wings of the scenery and that remains unknown to most people. "The triumphant city", of which Philippe De Commynes speaks in his memoirs, was born out of the interaction of its vital and material elements with the physical structure: both terms were indispensable. The architecture, the magnificence of the facades, the intense traffic of the waterways hark back to the trade of the past, the ways of the Orient, the ships loaded with merchandise and the liveliness of commerce. These found in the structure of the city the material expression of wealth. Today this is no longer inevitably so, and the very image of the city has been thrown into confusion.

The 19th century, then, has superimposed two images on the stratification in time of the urban structure and on its interpretation: one, a real one, which has modified in the forms of life, the *calli*, the buildings, in short the city as we see it today, and a literary one which through distorted reflections has penetrated deeply into international culture and has in a sense taken on a life of its own. And yet in few cities are past and present so closely interwoven and linked as in this one, where even the layout of the city itself is the same as it was five centuries ago. Each place bears the traces of some event, has been the witness to some act or has at least given rise to an anecdote, from each temporal segment the whole may be reconstructed. As the image of Venice alters so must the "use" of the city change no longer can it be an abstract place of recreation, of romantic associations and of counterfeit sentiments.

Greater attention ought to be paid to the rediscovery of the past: not only because through it the present is made more comprehensible, not only because each trace of history, each monument, each site acquires in this way its own precise features, but also because the way in which a future is imagined for this city must find its motivations in this very past.

Umberto Boccioni, The Grand Canal in Venice. Private collection.

Saint Mark's, the domes.

On the following pages
Plan of Venice.

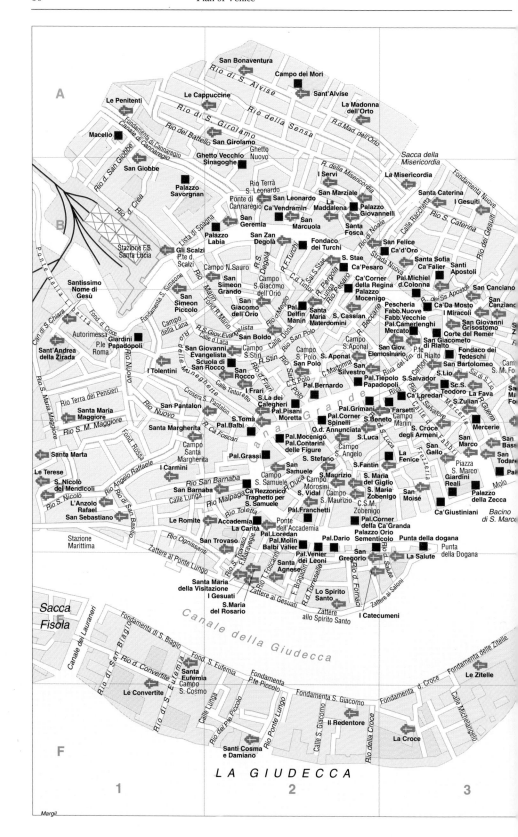

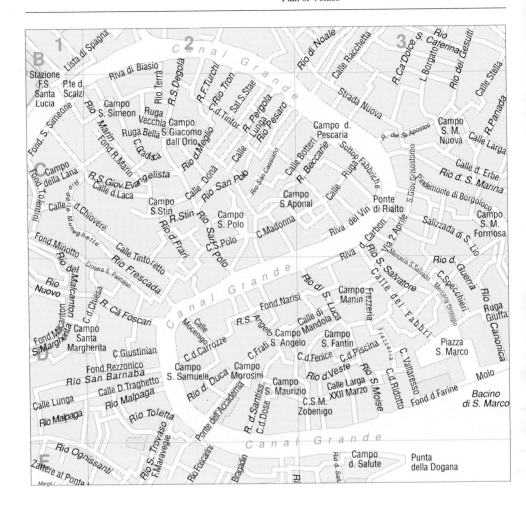

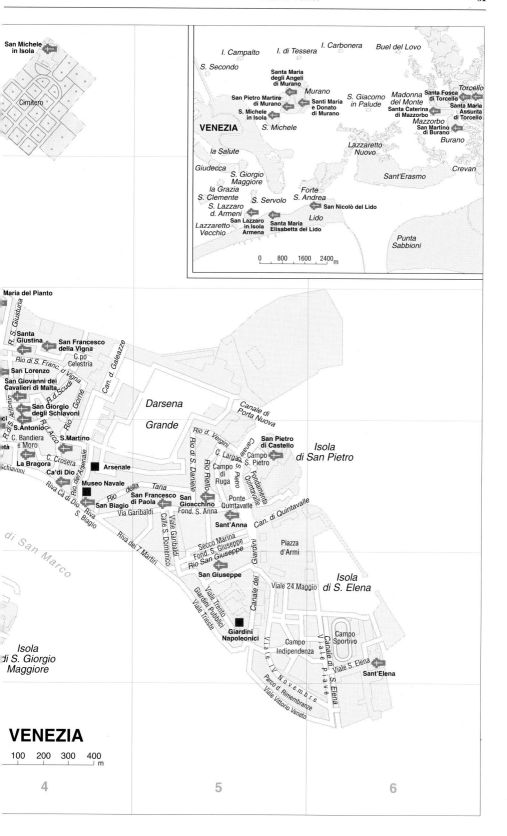

San Michele in Isola

Cimitero

I. Campalto
I. di Tessera
I. Carbonera
Buel del Lovo

S. Secondo

Santa Maria degli Angeli di Murano

Murano

San Pietro Martire di Murano
Santi Maria e Donato di Murano
S. Giacomo in Palude
Madonna del Monte
Santa Fosca di Torcello
Torcello

S. Michele in Isola

Santa Caterina di Mazzorbo
Santa Maria Assunta di Torcello

VENEZIA
S. Michele

Mazzorbo
San Martino di Burano

Burano

la Salute

Lazzaretto Nuovo

Giudecca
S. Giorgio Maggiore
la Grazia
S. Clemente
S. Servolo
Forte S. Andrea
San Nicolò del Lido

Sant'Erasmo

Crevan

S. Lazzaro d. Armeni
Lido

Lazzaretto Vecchio
San Lazzaro in Isola Armena
Santa Maria Elisabetta del Lido

Punta Sabbioni

0   800   1600   2400 m

Maria del Pianto

S. Giustina
Santa Giustina
San Francesco della Vigna
C.po Celestria
Rio di S. Franc.
Can. d. Galeazze

San Lorenzo

San Giovanni dei Cavalieri di Malta

R. di Scudi
R. Gorne
San Giorgio degli Schiavoni

R. d'Antonio

S.Antonio
C. Bandiera e Moro
tà
S.Martino
Darsena

Grande

Canale di Porta Nuova

La Bragora
C. Crosera
Ca' di Dio
Arsenale

Rio d. Vergini
Rio d. S. Daniele
C. Larga
Canale di S. Pietro
San Pietro di Castello

Campo S. Pietro

Isola di San Pietro

Museo Navale
Rio della Tana
San Francesco di Paola
San Gioacchino
Rio Riello
Campo di Ruga
Fondamenta Quintavalle
Ponte Quintavalle

San Biagio
Rio S. Biagio
Via Garibaldi
Fond. S. Anna
Can. di Quintavalle

Riva Cà di Dio
Riva dei 7 Martiri
Viale Garibaldi
Calle S. Domenico
Sant'Anna

di San Marco

Secco Marina
Fond. S. Giuseppe
Rio San Giuseppe

Piazza d'Armi

San Giuseppe
Viale 24 Maggio
Isola di S. Elena

Viale Trento
Giardini Pubblici
Viale Trieste

Canale dei Giardini

Giardini Napoleonici

Campo Indipendenza

Campo Sportivo

Campo S. Elena

Viale S. Elena
Sant'Elena

Isola di S. Giorgio Maggiore

Canale di S. Elena
Viale IV Novembre
Parco d. Rimembranze
Viale Vittorio Veneto

VENEZIA

100   200   300   400 m

4   5   6

Itineraries

The myth of Venice is alive today in its Square, which has always been and still is its consecration.

The visitor in a hurry often visits the central part of San Marco, thinking that he has seen Venice.

Even the official sign-posting from Piazzale Roma and the railway station often indicates no more than the direction of St. Mark's.

The rest of the city is seen as something that has to be crossed in order to get to the places that have been delegated to represent the whole.

Even those who are opposed to this partial vision of the city describe the other areas and monuments as "lesser Venice".

There are a thousand places, monuments, squares, churches and schools, filled with genuine treasures that have been neglected (and sometimes removed) on the grounds of this prejudice that is shared by residents and visitors alike.

And yet the Ghetto, the church of San Nicolò dei Mendicoli, the Scuola di San Rocco, the Frari and Santi Giovanni e Paolo are places that in themselves would justify a trip to Venice.

Even on the days when the influx of visitors to the city is at its greatest, when the streets are crowded with inattentive and tired groups of tourists, a few metres away from the official itineraries lies a silent and unknown city.

The fact is that any place, any little alley or part of this extraordinary city, can yield a discovery, perhaps the sight of a detail or a reflection, to the attentive visitors.

For Venice is above all a unique place, an endless series of surprises and sensations to be discovered or revisited.

The pages that follow present a series of "alternative" itineraries, as it is now customary to call them, but only because the official itineraries are so arbitrary.

These itineraries take in the whole of the city and its monuments, but they will also give to visitor a new and more realistic vision of Venice. Obviously they do not ignore St Mark's and the central area, but at the same time they are intended as an invitation to anyone who is interested to establish a more personal and direct relationship with the city, with its history and with its monuments.

Side page
Frari, apse, detail.

Itinerary 1
Piazzale Roma - Railway -
Fondamenta Nuove

1. Papadopoli Gardens
2. San Nicola da Tolentino
3. San Simeon Piccolo
4. Bridge of the Scalzi
5. Church of the Scalzi
6. San Geremia -
   Palazzo Labia
7. Palazzo Savorgnan
8. San Giobbe
9. Slaughterhouse
10. Penitenti
11. Old ghetto - Synagogue
12. New ghetto -
    San Girolamo
13. Campo dei Mori -
    Sant'Alvise
14. Madonna dell'Orto
15. Abbey of La Misericordia
16. Santa Caterina
17. Church of the Jesuits
    (ex Crociferi)

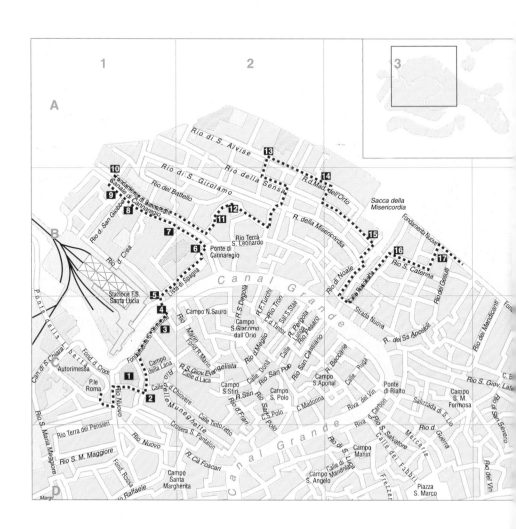

Papadopoli Gardens.   *La Misericordia.*
Entrance on the rio Nuovo.

Itinerary 2
Railway - San Marco

1. Church of the Scalzi
2. San Geremia -
   Palazzo Labia
3. Bridge of Spires
   (Ponte delle Guglie)
4. San Leonardo
5. San Marcuola -
   Ca' Vendramin
6. La Maddalena
7. Santa Fosca - Palazzo
   Giovannelli
8. San Felice
9. Ca' d'oro
10. Santa Sophia
11. Santi Apostoli - Ca' Falier
12. San Giovanni Crisostomo
13. Corte del Remer
14. Fontego dei Tedeschi
15. San Bartolomeo
16. San Salvatore -
    Scuola di San Teodoro
17. La Fava
18. Haberdasheries
    (Mercerie) - San Giuliano

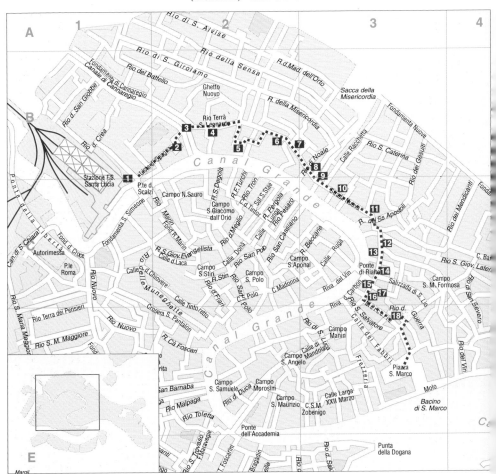

San Geremia, façade facing rio di Cannaregio.

La Maddalena, view from the canal of the same name.

Itinerary 3
**Piazzale Roma - Rialto
and environs**

1. San Nicola da Tolentino
2. San Rocco
3. Scuola di San Rocco
4. Frari
5. San Giovanni Evangelista
6. San Simeon Grande
7. San Zan Degolà
8. San Giacomo dell'Orio
9. San Stae
10. Santa Maria Mater
   Domini - Ca' Pesaro
11. Ca' Corner della Regina -
   Palazzo Mocenigo
12. San Cassiano
13. Fish-market - Fabbriche
   Nuove - Fabbriche
   Vecchie - Palazzo
   dei Camerlenghi -
   San Giacomo di Rialto -
   Rialto
14. San Silvestro
15. Sant'Aponal
16. San Polo

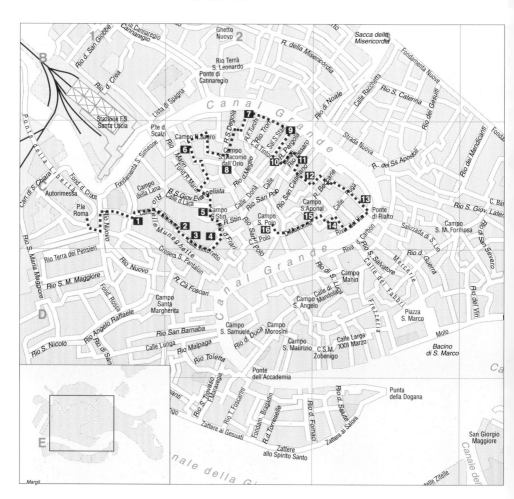

San Simeon Grande, façade.

San Giacometo, façade.

**Itinerary 4
Piazzale Roma - San Marco
by way of the Zattere**

1. San Pantalon
2. Santa Margherita
3. Carmini
4. Ognissanti - Eremite
5. San Trovaso
6. Santa Maria del Rosario
   (Gesuati)
7. Sant'Agnese
8. Spirito Santo
9. Salt Storehouses - Point
   of the Customs
10. Santa Maria della Salute
11. San Gregorio
12. Palazzo Dario -
    Guggenheim Foundation
13. Academy
14. San Vidal
15. Santo Stefano
16. San Maurizio
17. Santa Maria del Giglio
18. San Moisè

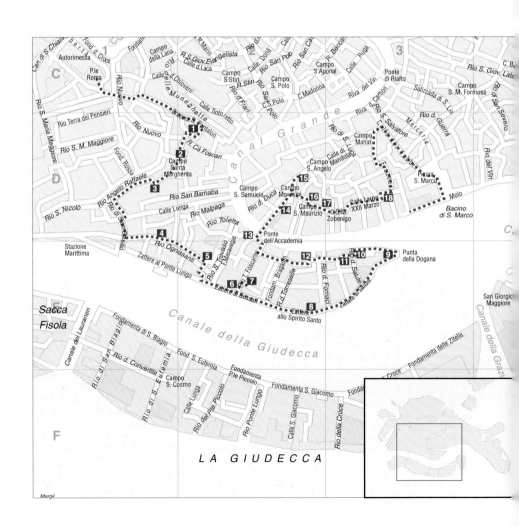

Gesuati, interior.

Church of the Eremite, façade.

Itinerary 5
Piazzale Roma - San Marco-
Piazzale Roma

1. San Rocco
2. Frari
3. San Tomà - Scuola dei
   Calegheri - Ca' Foscari
4. San Barnaba
5. Ca' Rezzonico - Ferry
   for San Samuele
6. San Samuele
7. Santo Stefano
8. San Fantin - La Fenice -
   Scala del Bovolo
9. San Marco
10. Ca' Giustinian
11. San Moisè
12. Santa Maria del Giglio
13. San Maurizio

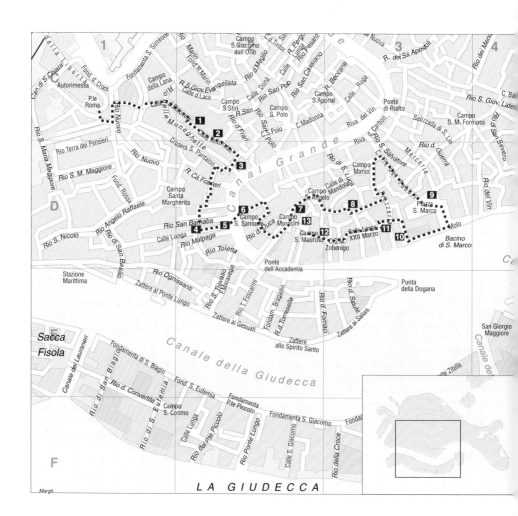

San Tomà. Marble lunette depicting the Virgin Mary and Worshippers.

Frari, Santissima Trinità, cloister.

Itinerary 6
**San Marco - Piazzale Roma
for San Giorgio and
Giudecca**

1. San Giorgio
2. Zitelle
3. Il Redentore
4. Sant'Eufemia
5. San Sebastiano
6. Angelo Raffaele
7. San Nicolò dei Mendicoli
8. Terese

*San Giorgio, church
and campanile.*

*San Nicolò dei Mendicoli,
the church from the corner
of the rio delle Terese.*

Itinerary 7
San Marco - Arsenal -
San Marco

1. Pietà
2. San Biagio -
   Naval Museum
3. Napoleonic Gardens
4. San Pietro di Castello
5. Sant'Anna -
   San Francesco di Paola
   Via Garibaldi
6. Arsenal
7. San Martino
8. La Bragora
9. San Giorgio dei Greci -
   Sant'Antonino
10. San Zaccaria
11. San Giovanni in Oleo

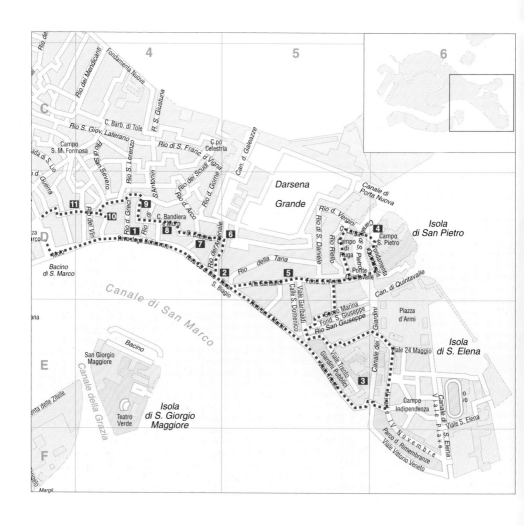

San Giovanni in Bragora, façade.

San Biagio, façade.

Itinerary 8
**San Marco - Fondamenta
Nuove - Murano**

1. Santi Filippo e Giacomo
2. Santa Maria Formosa
3. Querini Stampalia
4. San Lorenzo
5. San Giorgio dei Greci
6. San Giorgio
   degli Schiavoni
7. San Francesco
   della Vigna
8. Santa Giustina
9. Ospedaletto
10. Santi Giovanni e Paolo -
    Scuola di San Marco
11. Church of the Miracoli -
    San Canziano
12. San Michele

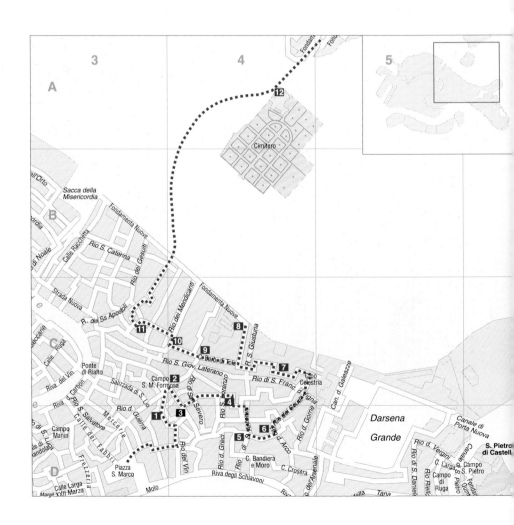

*San Francesco della Vigna,
cloister.*

*San Giovanni e Paolo,
portal.*

Itinerary 9
Grand Canal (aboard a line steamer)

1. San Simeon Piccolo
2. Gli Scalzi
3. San Geremia - Palazzo Labia
4. San Marcuola
5. Fontego dei Turchi
6. Ca' Vendramin-Calergi
7. San Stae
8. Ca' Pesaro
9. Ca' Corner della Regina
10. Ca' d'Oro
11. Palazzo Michiel della Colonna
12. Ca' Da Mosto
13. Fabbriche Nuove on Rialto - Market
14. Palazzo dei Camerlenghi
15. Fontego dei Tedeschi
16. Ca' Dolfin - Manin

17. Ca' Loredan
18. Ca' Farsetti
19. Palazzo Grimani
20. Palazzo Tiepolo-Papadopoli
21. Palazzo Bernardo
22. Palazzo Pisani Moretta
23. Palazzo Corner-Spinelli
24. Palazzo Balbi
25. Palazzo Mocenigo - Palazzo Contarini delle Figure
26. Ca' Foscari
27. Palazzo Grassi
28. Ca' Rezzonico
29. San Samuele
30. Academy - Campo della Carità
31. Palazzo Franchetti
32. Palazzo Loredan - Palazzo Molin Balbi-Valier
33. Palazzo Venier dei Leoni
34. Palazzo Dario

35. Palazzo Corner della Ca' Granda
36. Palazzo Orio Sementicolo
37. Santa Maria della Salute
38. Ca' Giustinian
39. Point of the Customs
40. Royal Gardens
41. Palazzo della Zecca
42. Doges' Palace

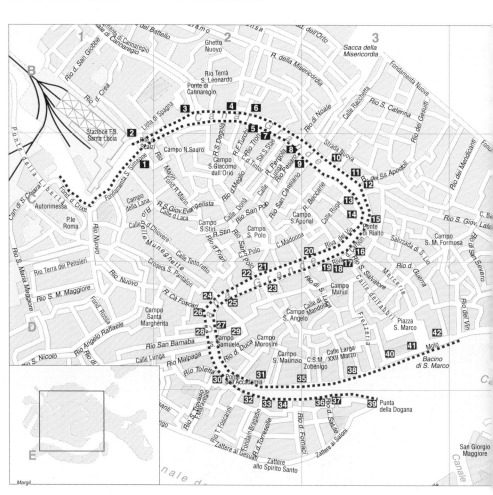

Fondaco dei Turchi.

Scalzi, façade.

Bibliography

Beltrami, *La popolazione veneziana dalla fine del XVI sec. alla caduta della Repubblica*, Cedam 1954.

Berengo, *La Società veneta alla fine del '700*, Sansoni 1956.

Luzzato, *Storia economica di Venezia dall'XI al XVI secolo*, Centro Internazionale Arti e Costume 1961.

Lorenzetti, *Venezia ed il suo estuario*, Lint 1974.

A.A.V.V., *Storia della Cultura Veneta*, Neri Pozza, 1976.

Bassi, *Palazzi di Venezia*, La Stamperia di Venezia 1976.

Perocco-Salvadori, *Civiltà di Venezia*, Giunti 1976.

Da Mosto, *I Dogi di Venezia*, Giunti 1977.

Romanelli, *Venezia nell'800*, Officina Edizioni 1977.

Samonà - Franzoi - Trincanato, *Piazza S. Marco, L'Architettura, la Storia, le funzioni*, Marsilio 1977.

Bettini, *Venezia, nascita di una città*, Electa 1978.

Lane, *Storia di Venezia*, Einaudi 1978.

Branca, *Storia della civiltà veneziana*, Sansoni 1979.

Brusatin, *Venezia del '700: stato, architettura, territorio*, Einaudi 1980.

Cozzi, *Stato, società e giustizia nella Repubblica Veneta*, Jouvence 1980.

Tucci, *Mercanti, navi, monete nel 500 veneziano*, Mulino 1981.

Crivellari, *Venezia*, Electa 1982.

Venezia nell'800, edited by Pavanello e Romanelli, 1983.

Bellavitis e Romanelli, *Le città della storia d'Italia: Venezia*, Laterza 1985.

Concina, *Venezia nell'età moderna*, Marsilio 1989.

Architettura e utopia nella Venezia del '500, edited by Puppi, Electa 1989.

Cooperman, *Il ghetto di Venezia*, Arsenale Ed. 1990.

Photographs
Archivio Electa, Milan.
The plans were executed
by Studio Margil.

Printed for Electa
by Fantonigrafica-Elemond Editori Associati